UPCYCLED

ACCESSORIES

UPCYCLED

ACCESSORIES
25 projects using repurposed plastic

Tracie Lampe

NORTH LIGHT BOOKS
CINCINNATI, OHIO

www.fwmedia.com

15 14 13 12 11 10   5 4 3 2 1
2010

DISTRIBUTED IN CANADA BY FRASER DIRECT
100 Armstrong Avenue
Georgetown, ON, Canada L7G 5S4
Tel: (905) 877-4411

DISTRIBUTED IN THE U.K. AND EUROPE
 BY DAVID & CHARLES
Brunel House, Newton Abbot, Devon, TQ12 4PU,
England
Tel: (+44) 1626 323200, Fax: (+44) 1626 323319
E-mail: postmaster@davidandcharles.co.uk

DISTRIBUTED IN AUSTRALIA BY CAPRICORN LINK
P.O. Box 704, S. Windsor NSW, 2756 Australia
Tel: (02) 4577-3555

Library of Congress Cataloging in Publication Data
Lampe, Tracie
  Upcycled accessories : 25 projects using repurposed
plastic / Tracie Lampe. -- 1st ed.
      p. cm.
  Includes index.
  ISBN-13: 978-1-60061-995-3 (pbk. : alk. paper)
  ISBN-10: 1-60061-995-9 (pbk. : alk. paper)
  1. Plastics craft. 2. Salvage (Waste, etc.) I. Title.
  TT297.L27 2010
  745.57--dc22
                        2009037123

Metric Conversion Chart

To convert	to	multiply by
Inches	Centimeters	2.54
Centimeters	Inches	0.4
Feet	Centimeters	30.5
Centimeters	Feet	0.03
Yards	Meters	0.9
Meters	Yards	1.1

Edited by Rachel Scheller

Cover designed by Rachael Smith
and Marissa Bowers

Layout designed by Rachael Smith

Production coordinated by Greg Nock

Photography by Christine Polomsky
and Al Parrish

Styling by Jan Nickum

fw
media

About the Author

Tracie Lampe lives in the friendly mitten state of Michigan with her wonderful husband, Mike, and two children, Nickolas and Shae. Her favorite place to be is at her home, where she fills her time with crafting and creating. Her recent obsession with recycling has taken over her life as well as the lives of her family. This is her first book.

Dedication

To Mike, my husband. Without you, I wouldn't have the courage to chase my dreams.

To my children, Nickolas and Shae. I love you both more than you can imagine.

To Dad, for the morning talks and for being a great dad.

To Tawnya, for being my long-distance cheerleader and BFF. Your unwavering encouragement and total understanding mean more than I could ever express.

To Becky, for being the best neighbor a person could have! Thanks for planting the seed that led me down this road.

To Lori, my muse. Thanks for your constant encouragement.

To my girls, Carrie, Brenda, Beth and Andrea, for always being there and accepting my handmade gifts with a smile.

To Girl Scouts of America, Heart of Michigan Council, for hosting the class that encouraged me to make a change.

Thanks to Tonia Davenport, for your guidance and help in this journey; Rachel Scheller, for being a fabulous editor and making every step a breeze; and Christine Polomsky, for putting up with me during photo shoot week.

To all my family and friends: I believe that every person is brought into our lives for a reason, and whether they stay forever or just a short time, we all learn something, good or bad. I am thankful for every one of you and everything that has led me to where I am today. I couldn't be more blessed.

Contents

Introduction

I was first inspired to recycle plastic by Candace Myshock, who taught a class hosted by the Girl Scouts called "Leave No Trace." Up to that point I hadn't recycled a thing and was contemplating getting a fourth trash can to hold our weekly trash. During this class, Candace talked about how long it takes trash to break down in a landfill and asked us if we could help eliminate this problem in some small way. I remember turning to my friend Becky and saying that I would start recycling right away. At first, I had no clue what could or couldn't go into a blue recycling bin, so my friend gave me a crash course.

After the first week of recycling, I had reduced our weekly trash from an overflowing three cans to less than one. My heart was filled with joy, and soon the act of recycling turned into the idea of creating things from the stuff in the blue bin. That year, our theme for Girl Scout camp was "Recycling, Reusing, Reducing," so my friend and I came up with different ways of incorporating trash into crafts to fit the theme. One of these crafts was a sitting mat (or "sit-upon" in Girl Scout-speak) made from fused plastic bags. I loved the concept so much that I started looking around the house for plastic I could fuse. Frozen veggie bags, cereal

bags, cheese bags, paper towel wrapping, toilet paper wrapping—I was amazed at the amount of plastic I was finding throughout the house. Unfortunately, it couldn't be recycled because it didn't have a number on it. I kept thinking about how long it took for plastic like this to break down, and suddenly it occurred to me that the plastic I was throwing away could be recycled in a different way—in the form of accessories!

It's not always easy to live a "green" life. (I do sometimes forget to turn the water off while brushing my teeth.) However, if we can each change just one thing about our current lifestyle,

wouldn't that be great? This book is one way to start thinking about those changes. Keep your plastic bags out of the trash—or even the blue bin—by fusing and reusing them!

How cool would it be to give your BFF a handmade bag from recycled plastic? It only costs you time and love, and you would be doing a bit to save our planet. If we all do our part, even in simple, small ways, the result will be bigger than we can imagine.

Materials and Tools

Materials

Plastic: Don't limit your plastic choices to grocery store bags! There's an entire mountain of plastic that gets thrown away on a daily basis: food packaging, newspaper sleeves, bottle caps, water bottle labels . . . the possibilities are endless. The projects in this book go beyond using plastic bags and will give you plenty of ideas for items to use.

Parchment paper: I prefer to use unbleached silicone-coated parchment paper made by Source Atlantique. It is manufactured without chlorine bleach, which prevents chemicals from being dumped into rivers, lakes and streams. As a bonus, it can go in the compost bin when you're finished!

Felt fabric: Any felt fabric will work for the projects in this book. Environmentally friendly Eco-Felt comes in an array of colors and is so soft, you wouldn't even know it was made from plastic bottles! Soft, fluffy and eco-friendly—what more could you want?

Paints: Acrylic paint, which is essentially made from plastic, is versatile and comes in so many colors. When choosing paint pens, make sure they are acrylic as well. I don't recommend spray paint because it tends to flake off after it has dried.

Tools

Vintage iron: I recommend using a vintage iron to fuse plastic and assist in plastic appliqué. This tool is ideal because it doesn't have steam holes or a Teflon coating. You can pick one up at an antique store or flea market or on eBay. And of course, if you're going to use an iron, you are going to need an ironing board, too.

Sewing machine: I use a Husqvarna Viking, but any machine that has a zigzag stitch will work. When sewing with fused plastic, I find that the zigzag stitch works best; all of the projects in this book use the zigzag stitch.

A machine equipped with a roller foot is also helpful. A roller foot is typically used for sewing leather, velvet or uneven layers of fabric, but it seems to work great on fused plastic, too!

Scissors: I don't use fabric scissors for fused plastic. Instead, I use a pair of Fiskars that can be purchased at any local craft or discount store. They are fabulous and never seem to dull.

Embroidery scissors: I use these to trim threads on sewn pieces, making the finished project look neater.

Magnetic pin holder: This is a magnetic dish that holds tight to your pins so they don't scatter all over the floor.

Straight pins: I use 0.5mm fine glass head pins instead of regular straight pins because they poke through the plastic fabric like butter and make your life so much easier.

Tape measure: I have an ample supply of small tape measures so I can accurately cut pieces of fused plastic, ribbon, felt and what-ever else is going on my project. Remember the golden rule: Measure twice, cut once!

Techniques

Preparing Plastic Bags

Materials

※ 3 plastic shopping bags (works best if they are all from the same store)

Tools

※ scissors

1 Flatten out three plastic bags and stack them. Cut off the tops and bottoms of the bags.

2 Pull the bags apart and smooth out all folds and wrinkles.

 **tip** When trimming the tops and bottoms of plastic bags, save the resulting scraps for other projects, like the *Robot Plushie* (see page 112) or the *Large Camera Bag* (see page 56). If you don't need the scraps, make sure to recycle them.

Fusing Plastic Bags

Materials

❋ prepared stack of plastic bags

Tools

❋ iron, ironing board, parchment paper

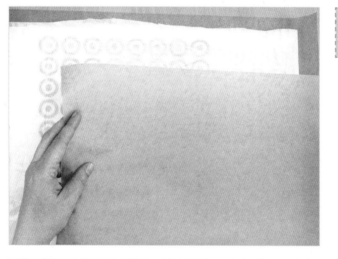

1 Sandwich the stack of bags between two sheets of parchment paper. Set the iron to the medium or wool setting. Adjust to a cooler temperature if necessary.

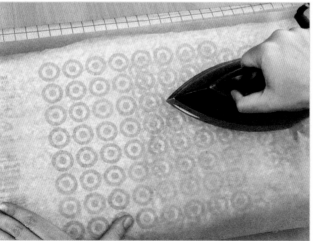

2 Start ironing in the middle of the stack and work to the edges. Make sure the plastic cools before checking to see if it's fused. Flip the stack over and repeat the process.

Allow the plastic to cool before removing the parchment paper.

Plastic Appliqué

Materials
- ✳ fused plastic, used black garbage bag

Tools
- ✳ iron, ironing board, scissors

1 Cut out letters from a used black garbage bag (or any thin, unfused plastic). Place the letters onto a piece of fused plastic.

2 Place a sheet of parchment paper over the letters. Iron on this side.

3 After the plastic has cooled for a few seconds, remove the parchment paper.

Fabric Appliqué

Materials
* ❋ felt scraps, fused plastic

Tools
* ❋ iron, ironing board, scissors, sewing machine with leather foot attachment, straight pins

1 Cut out shapes or letters from the felt scraps. Pin each felt piece to a piece of fused plastic with straight pins.

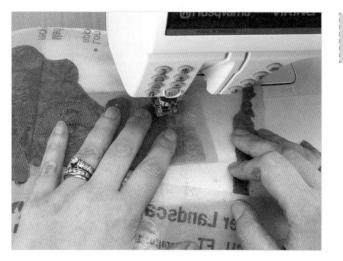

2 With the sewing machine, sew each felt piece onto the plastic using zigzag stitch.

Crayon Shavings

Materials
❋ clear plastic bags, crayons

Tools
❋ iron, ironing board,
parchment paper,
small grater

 Use the small grater to grate crayon bits into shavings. Separate different colors into color families (reds, greens, yellows, etc.) for storage.

2 Disperse desired colors of crayon shavings evenly throughout a clear plastic bag. Flatten the bag to prepare for fusing.

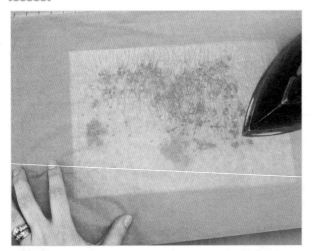

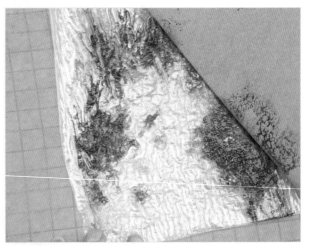

3 Place another clear plastic bag on top of the one that has crayon shavings in it. Sandwich the bags in parchment paper. Iron one side and then the other.

4 After the plastic has cooled for a few seconds, remove the parchment paper.

Permanent Markers

Materials

✳ permanent markers,
  unfused plastic bags

Tools

✳ iron, ironing board,
  parchment paper

1 Using permanent markers, draw a design onto a stack of unfused plastic bags.

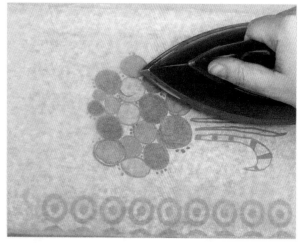

2 Sandwich the stack of bags in parchment paper. Iron on one side and then the other. This will set the design into the plastic.

3 After the plastic has cooled for a few seconds, remove the parchment paper.

Tulle

Materials
* clear plastic bags, plastic tulle

Tools
* iron, ironing board, scissors

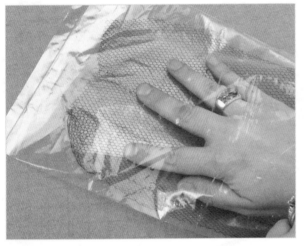

1 Cut a piece of tulle and slide it into a clear plastic bag. Place another clear plastic bag on top of the first one.

2 Sandwich the clear plastic bags and tulle in parchment paper. Iron on one side and then the other.

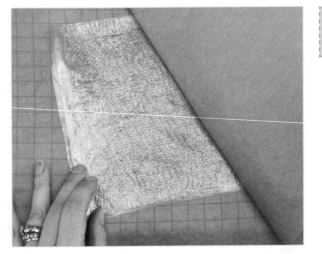

3 After the plastic has cooled for a few seconds, remove the parchment paper.

Collage

Materials

✳ assorted colors of plastic packaging, fused plastic fabric

Tools

✳ iron, ironing board, parchment paper, scissors, sewing machine (optional)

1 Cut out different shapes and collage elements from unfused plastic and place onto a piece of fused plastic.

2 Place a sheet of parchment paper over the collage. Iron on one side.

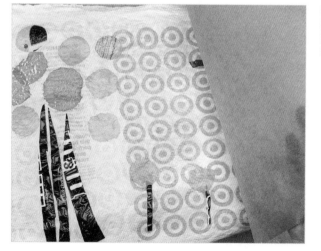

3 After the plastic has cooled for a few seconds, remove the parchment paper. If you choose, you can also zigzag stitch around the collage elements to secure them.

Confetti

Materials
✳ clear plastic bags, flagging tape

Tools
✳ iron, ironing board, scissors, parchment paper

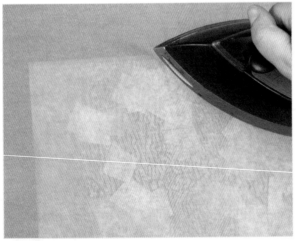

1 Cut the flagging tape into small pieces.

2 Slide the flagging tape pieces into a clear plastic bag and disperse evenly.

3 Place another plastic bag on top of the first bag. Sandwich the clear plastic bags in parchment paper. Iron on one side and then the other.

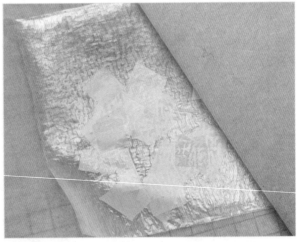

4 After the plastic has cooled for a few seconds, remove the parchment paper.

Paints

Materials
✶ acrylic paint, clear sealer, fused plastic

Tools
✶ paintbrush

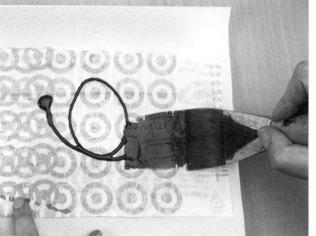

1 Paint a piece of fused plastic with acrylic paint. Let the paint dry.

2 Apply a clear sealer over the painted plastic fabric. Let it dry.

Paint Pens

Materials

✳ fused plastic, paint pens

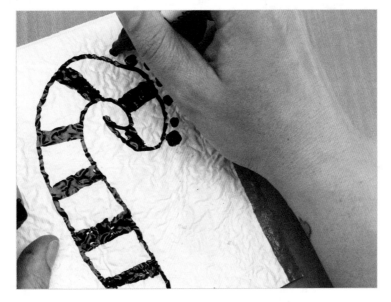

Using paint pens, draw a design onto a piece of fused plastic. Let the design dry.

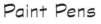

Paint pens come in a variety of colors; don't hesitate to apply some truly wacky and wonderful designs to your projects. Note that if paint pens are used prior to sewing, the sewing machine might "scuff" the design, so it's usually best to apply the design to the finished project.

Stencils

Materials

❋ acrylic paint, fused plastic

Tools

❋ paintbrush or foam brush, stencils

1 Place a stencil onto a piece of fused plastic. Apply paint to the insides of the stencil with a paintbrush or foam brush.

2 Carefully remove the stencil to avoid smearing the paint. Let the paint dry.

23

Stamps

Materials

* ※ StazOn permanent ink, unfused plastic bags

Tools

* ※ iron, ironing board, parchment paper, rubber stamp

 1 Apply permanent ink to a rubber stamp and press the stamp firmly onto a stack of unfused plastic bags.

2 Sandwich the bags in parchment paper. Iron on one side and then the other.

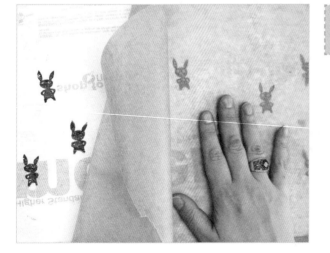

 3 After the plastic has cooled for a few seconds, remove the parchment paper.

Striping

Materials

✦ colorful plastic packaging

Tools

✦ iron, ironing board, scissors, sewing machine

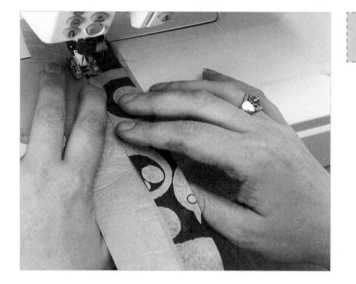

 **1** Fuse several different types of colorful plastic packaging and cut the pieces into 1" (3cm) strips. Sew the strips together lengthwise, overlapping them approximately ¼" (6mm).

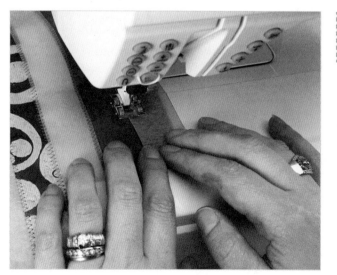

 2 Continue sewing strips together to achieve the desired size.

Projects

I am always studying items made with fabric, trying to see if I can design something similar using fused plastic.

It's so much fun to see what I can come up with. The projects in this book are ones I have designed so far, and I am thinking of more everyday. It's so gratifying to craft something handmade, but even more so to make it out of materials that would otherwise go to the landfill. I hope that as you try your hand at these projects, or use my techniques to design your own, you will feel the same joy as I do.

Before you head to the beach, be sure to whip up a *Tote Bag* (see page 52) for all your beach stuff. It's not only stylish, but waterproof, too! Or downsize the *Tote Bag* and make a recycled gift bag for a birthday gift. Personalize it with the recipient's name for that special added touch. For your next dinner party, make custom plastic *Placemats* (see page 76) for each guest. A *Shower Essentials Caddy*, *Shower Cap*, *Shower Slippers* and a *Clothing Caddy* (see pages 84, 88, 90 and 92, respectively) will make shower time easier for your little one as she heads off to summer camp.

I know I can't save the world alone, but maybe together we can make a difference. These projects are a great way to start.

Neon Wallet

I first made this wallet out of a Wonder Bread wrapper and gave it to my son for Christmas. He loved it, of course, but never saw past the novelty of owning a wallet made from trash. I get a kick out of the fact that he's helping the environment and doesn't even know it!

Techniques used:
Fusing Plastic Bags, page 13
Confetti, page 20

Finished measurements:
3¾" × 3½" (10cm × 9cm)

Materials list

Plastic
- ❋ clear plastic bags
- ❋ neon green colored newspaper sleeve
- ❋ neon pink shopping bag

Tools
- ❋ iron
- ❋ ironing board
- ❋ measuring tape
- ❋ scissors
- ❋ sewing machine
- ❋ straight pins

Templates
- ❋ Wallet ID pocket, page 120

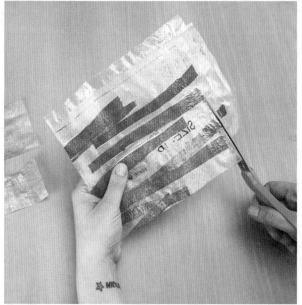

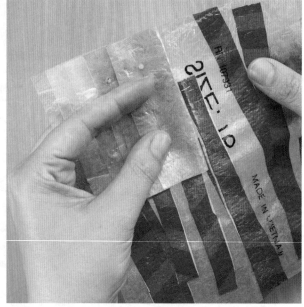

1 Refer to the confetti technique to prepare the pink and green pieces of fused plastic. Cut a 7¾" × 6½" (20cm × 17cm) piece of pink plastic for the wallet base. Cut two 3¾" × 3½" (10cm × 9cm) pieces of green plastic for the wallet pockets. Use the template to cut an ID pocket from the green plastic.

2 Fold the wallet base in half lengthwise, and then in half again widthwise. Trim to make the edges even.

3 Fold each wallet pocket up 3" (8cm) widthwise. Line up the pockets so the edges are about ½" (1cm) apart and pin into place.

4 Pin the wallet pockets in place along the right inside edge of the wallet. Pin the ID pocket to the left inside edge.

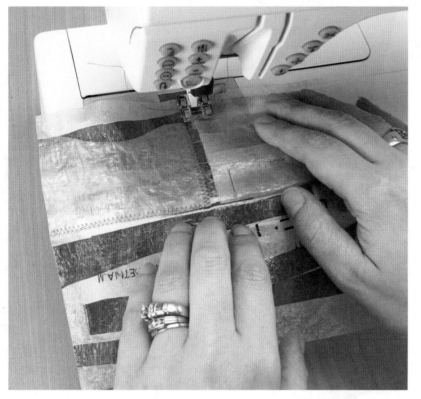

5 With the wallet base completely unfolded, sew the wallet pockets and ID pocket to the inside of the wallet.

6 Fold the wallet base along the lengthwise crease and pin in place. Sew along the shorter sides of the wallet.

Snap Coin Purse

Remember that snap coin purse you bought at a souvenir shop on vacation with your parents? This is my version of it. It's made from plastic, not leather, and it's much more gratifying to pull this one out of my purse to get some quarters for the bubble gum machine.

Technique used:
Fusing Plastic Bags, page 13

Finished measurements:
4" × 3½" (10cm × 9cm)

Materials

Plastic
* plastic snack packaging

Notions
* felt scraps
* 3½" × 15mm internal flex frame

Tools
* iron
* ironing board
* measuring tape
* scissors
* sewing machine
* straight pins

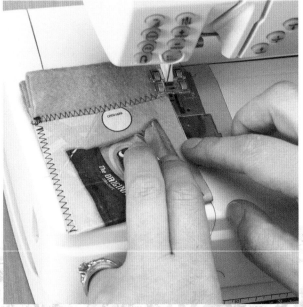

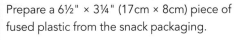

1 Prepare a 6½" × 3¼" (17cm × 8cm) piece of fused plastic from the snack packaging.

2 Cut two 3¼" × 2¼" (8cm × 6cm) pieces of felt. Fold each piece in half lengthwise and pin.

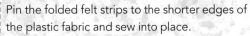

3 Pin the folded felt strips to the shorter edges of the plastic fabric and sew into place.

4 Fold the plastic in half, wrong sides together. Sew the sides of the plastic fabric to create a pouch. Do not sew over the felt pieces.

5 Insert one side of an internal flex frame into each of the felt pieces. Connect the frame on the other end.

tip

An internal flex frame will make your coin purse really "snap," but they aren't as easy to find as you might think. Search for *3.5" internal flex frame* online—this will yield results!

Purse Pouch

I hate when I can't find my lip gloss in my purse, especially while I'm driving. By the time I find it, my entire purse is dumped out on the passenger seat! I whipped up this purse pouch so I could keep all of my beauty essentials at my fingertips—and no one gets hurt while I'm driving!

Technique used:
Confetti, page 20

Finished measurements:
6½" × 4" × 1¼" (17cm × 10cm × 3cm)

Materials

Plastic
- ✳ clear plastic bags
- ✳ silver plastic scraps

Notions
- ✳ Velcro dots

Tools
- ✳ ink pen
- ✳ iron
- ✳ ironing board
- ✳ measuring tape
- ✳ scissors
- ✳ sewing machine
- ✳ straight edge
- ✳ straight pins

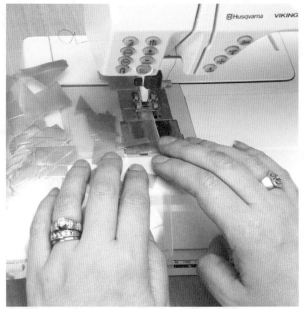

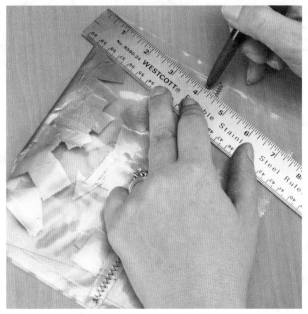

1   Refer to the confetti technique to create a 11¾" × 8¼" (30cm × 21cm) piece of fused plastic using the clear bags and silver scraps. Fold in one short edge ¼" (6mm) and sew down to create a finished edge.

2   Starting with the finished edge, fold the plastic 8½" (22cm) up with the right sides together, creating a 4" (10cm) deep pocket. Draw sewing lines along the sides at a slight angle so the bottom of the pouch will be wider than the top. Sew along the lines. Trim the fabric to within ¼" (6mm) of the seams. Trim the flap along the sewing lines.

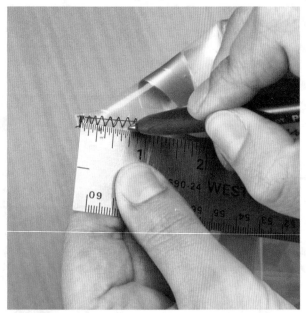

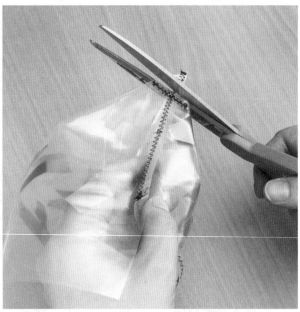

3   Fold the pouch to create points at both ends of the bottom. Measure ¾"(2cm) down from each point and mark. Sew across these marks to create a triangle at each point.

4   Cut each point ¼" (6mm) from the seam. Turn the bag right side out.

38

5 Fold the sides and top of the flap in ¼" (6mm) and sew down to create finished edges.

6 Adhere the Velcro dots to the inside of the flap and the pocket.

Striped Cell Phone Case

My cell phone is always taking a nap at the bottom of my purse, next to my lip gloss. When it rings, I can never find it underneath all the other things I carry around with me, and I end up missing the call. I made this cute and functional cell phone holder so that I can always pick up when my hubby and kids need me!

Techniques used:
Fusing Plastic Bags, page 13
Striping, page 25

Finished measurements:
6" × 4" (15cm × 10cm)

Materials

Plastic
* colorful plastic packaging

Notions
* ¼" (6mm) double-fold bias tape
* felt scrap
* Velcro dots

Tools
* iron
* ironing board
* measuring tape
* scissors
* sewing machine
* straight pins

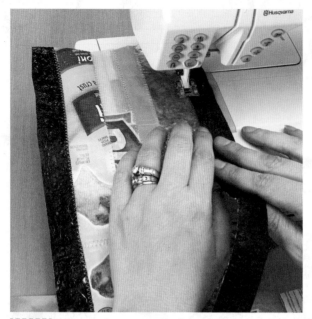

1 Refer to the striping technique to create a 10" × 8" (25cm × 20cm) striped piece of fused plastic using various colors of plastic packaging.

2 Cut a 9½" × 6" (24cm × 15cm) piece of striped plastic. Cut a 6½" × 6" (17cm × 15cm) piece of felt.

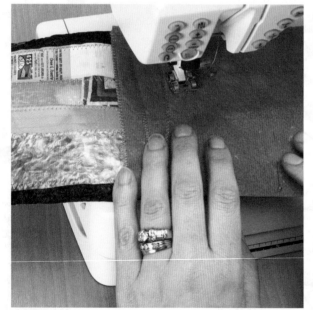

3 Pin the felt to one side of the striped plastic, aligning it with one of the shorter edges. Sew back and forth across the stripes to attach the felt to the plastic. The felt will line the inside of the pouch.

4 Fold the entire piece in half lengthwise so the top edges of the flap meet. Round the corners of the flap.

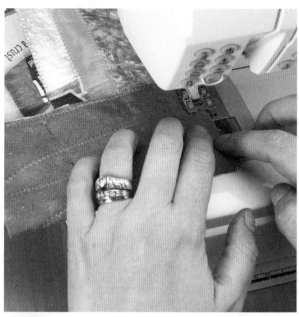

5 Cut 20" (51cm) of ¼" (6mm) wide bias tape. Pin the bias tape to the plastic, starting halfway up the fabric lining, around the rounded edge, and halfway down the other side of the fabric lining. Sew the bias tape to the flap.

6 Fold the fabric-lined portion in half widthwise so the fabric is facing outward. Sew the edges.

7 Turn the holder so the fabric is on the inside of the pocket. Adhere a Velcro dot to the inside of the flap and the pocket.

Spiral Clutch

Need a small purse to carry your moola and lip gloss while you're out with the girls? Make yourself this clutch and customize it to match your outfit. Now everyone at girls' night will want you to make them one. Remember to bring some paper and a pen to take orders!

Techniques used:
Fusing Plastic Bags, page 13
Permanent Markers, page 17

Finished measurements:
8¼" × 5" (21cm × 13cm)

Materials

Plastic
* plastic shopping bag

Notions
* felt fabric
* Velcro dots

Tools
* iron
* ironing board
* sewing machine
* scissors
* straight pins
* permanent markers

Templates
* clutch form, page 124
* clutch pocket, page 125

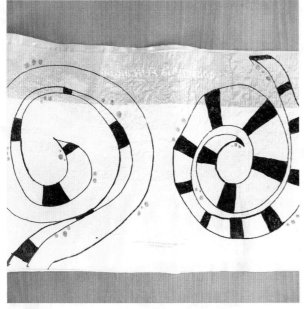

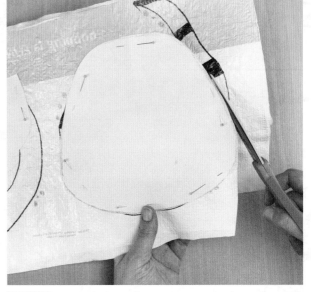

1 Prepare a piece of fused plastic from the thick plastic shopping bag. Refer to the permanent markers technique to draw a custom design onto the plastic.

2 Using the templates, cut one clutch pocket and one clutch form from the fused plastic. Cut two clutch pockets from the felt.

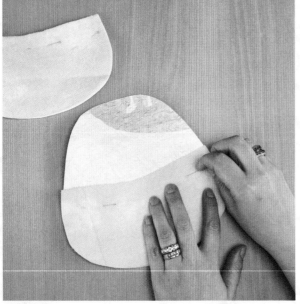

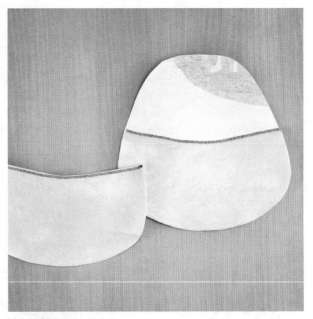

3 Pin one felt piece to the wrong side of the plastic clutch pocket and one felt piece to the wrong side of the clutch form.

4 Sew along the uncurved, flat edge of the clutch pocket. Sew along the edge of the clutch form where the felt stops and the plastic begins. On both pieces, leave the curved edges unsewn.

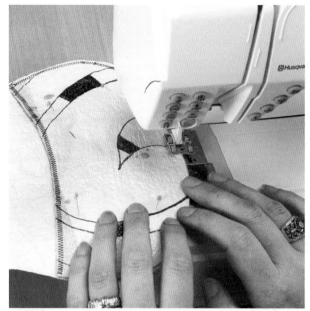

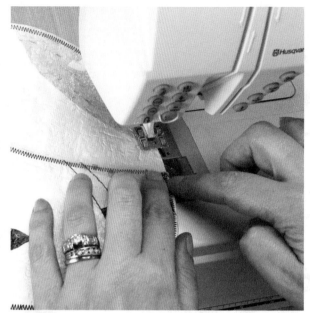

5 Match the clutch pocket to the clutch form, felt sides together. Pin in place, and then sew around the bottom half of the clutch form. Trim the edges of the plastic to within ¼" (6mm) of the seam to create a neater finish.

6 Sew around the entire clutch form. Fold the top of the clutch form down to create a flap.

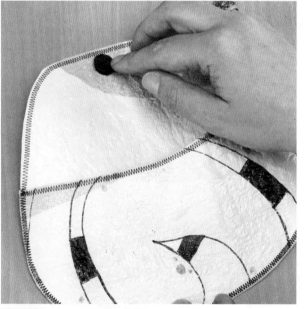

7 Adhere a Velcro dot to the inside of the flap and the pocket.

Lunch Bag

These days, we all need to cut back a bit. One of the easiest ways to do this is to start packing a lunch for work rather than eating out. But don't spend money on a new lunch bag or box; instead, make this one out of some plastic trash!

Techniques used:
Fusing Plastic Bags, page 13
Paint Pens, page 22

Finished measurements:
10" × 7¼" (25cm × 18cm)

Materials

Plastic
* white shopping bags

Notions
* 1" (3cm) wide nylon webbing
* paint pens
* Velcro dots

Tools
* iron
* ironing board
* measuring tape
* scissors
* sewing machine
* straight pins

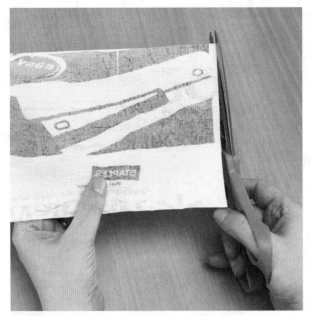

1 Cut pieces of fused plastic in the following sizes: 7" × 6" (18cm × 15cm) for the bottom, 12½" × 7¼" (32cm × 18cm) for the back, 9½" × 7" (24cm × 18cm) for the front, and two 9½" × 6" (24cm × 15cm) pieces for the sides.

2 Pin the front, back and side pieces to the edges of the bottom piece. Sew the pieces together where pinned.

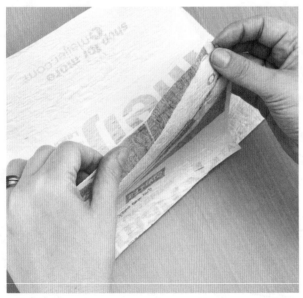

3 Pin the sides to the front and back pieces of the bag. Sew together where pinned.

4 The additional length of the back piece creates a flap. Fold the flap down over the front. Cut a 12" (30cm) piece of 1" (3cm) nylon webbing and burn the ends with a lighted match to prevent raveling. Pin the webbing to the back of the lunch bag where the flap fold begins. Sew the webbing into place to create a handle.

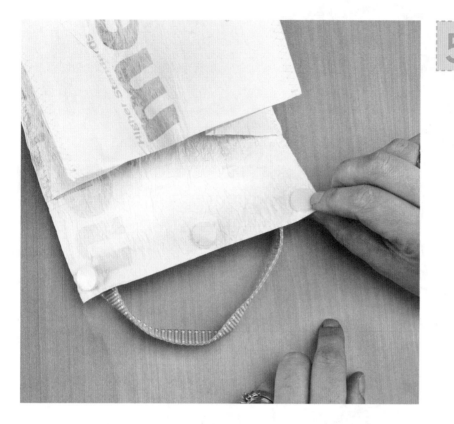

5 Adhere three Velcro dots to the inside flap and pocket of the lunch bag, spacing them evenly across.

6 Refer to the paint pens technique to create a design on the lunch bag.

Tote Bag

A tote bag made from upcycled plastic—what a great way to show your love for our planet by hanging one of these over your shoulder for all to see! You can even scale down the pattern and make gift bags for that last-minute birthday party. You'll not only save a few bucks, but you'll be the talk of the party with your oh-so-cool gift bag!

Techniques used:
Fusing Plastic Bags, page 13
Collage, page 19

Finished measurements:
18¼" × 14½"
(46cm × 37cm)

Materials

Plastic
- ✳ colorful plastic packaging
- ✳ 3 used white plastic garbage bags

Notions
- ✳ ½" (1mm) double-fold bias tape

- ✳ 1" (3cm) wide nylon webbing

Tools
- ✳ iron
- ✳ ironing board
- ✳ measuring tape

- ✳ pencil
- ✳ scissors
- ✳ sewing machine
- ✳ straight pins

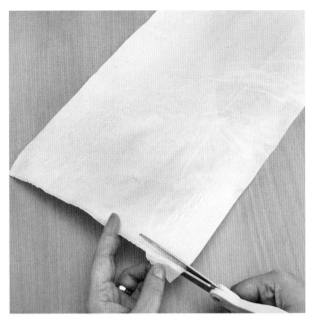

1 Prepare a piece of fused plastic from the three garbage bags. Cut three 20½" × 11¾" (52cm × 30cm) pieces from the fused plastic for the front, back and bottom of the bag.

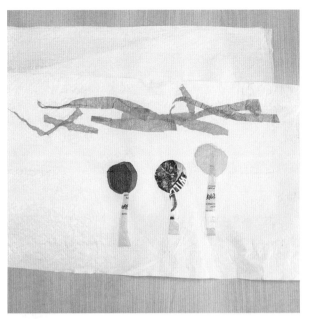

2 Refer to the collage technique to create a collage on the front piece of the bag.

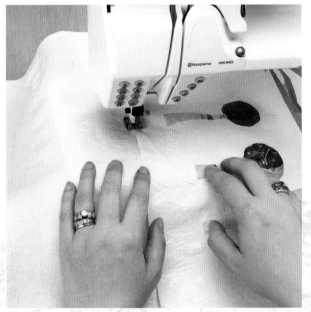

3 Sew the bottom piece to the bottom edge of the front piece. Sew the back piece to the other side of the bottom piece.

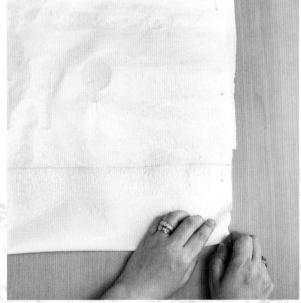

4 Fold the bag in half so the front and back pieces are facing, right sides together. Pin and sew each side.

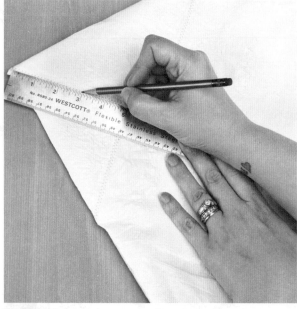

5 Fold the bag so the corners form points on the bottom. Measure 3" (8cm) down from each point and mark with a pencil.

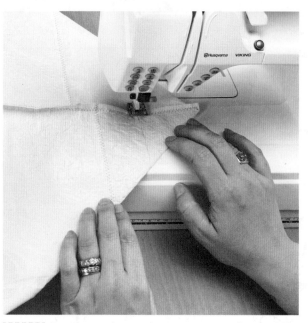

6 Sew across this mark to create a small triangle at each point.

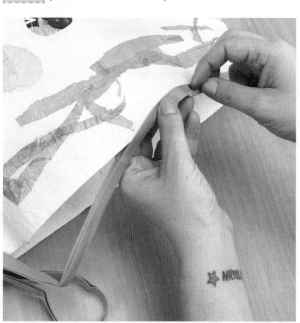

7 Turn the bag right side out. Measure enough ½" (1cm) double-fold bias tape to go around the top edge of the bag. Pin the tape into place and then sew.

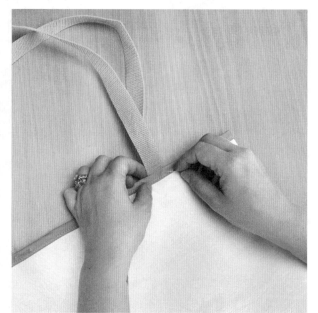

8 Cut two 28" (71cm) pieces of 1" (3cm) nylon webbing. Burn each end of the webbing pieces to prevent raveling. Pin one piece to the front of the bag and one to the back of the bag to create a handle on each side, positioning each end of the webbing about 5" (13cm) in from the side seams. Sew each strip to the bag, running over the strips several times for strength.

tip

The tote bag pattern is easily adjustable to fit your needs. Want a smaller or larger bag? Simply adjust the measurements of your front, back and bottom pieces, making sure they're all the same size. This "Wavy" bag, made using smaller pieces of fused plastic and the plastic appliqué technique, is perfect for carrying essentials.

Large Camera Bag

So you bought a fancy new camera and have nothing to carry it in, huh? Why not make a padded camera bag to protect it from the elements. There's even enough room for your film or an extra lens; you'll never be unprepared for picture-taking again!

Techniques used:
Fusing Plastic Bags, page 13
Striping, page 25

Finished measurements:
11" × 6½" × 5¾" (28cm × 17cm × 15cm)

Materials

Plastic
※ colorful plastic packaging
※ unfused plastic scraps
※ white shopping bags

Notions
※ 1" (3cm) wide nylon webbing
※ Velcro dots

Tools
※ iron
※ ironing board
※ measuring tape
※ pencil
※ scissors
※ sewing machine
※ straight pins

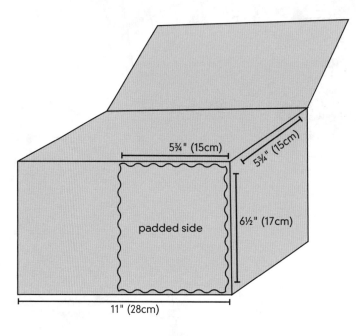

5¾" (15cm)

5¾" (15cm)

6½" (17cm)

padded side

11" (28cm)

 1 Prepare several large pieces of fused plastic from the white shopping bags. Cut six 6½" × 5¾" (17cm × 15cm) small bag pieces, three 11" × 6½" (28cm × 17cm) large bag pieces, one 10" × 4¾" (25cm × 12cm) large divider piece and one 6¼" × 4¾" (16cm × 12cm) small divider piece from the fused plastic.

2 Pin two of the small side pieces together. Pin a small side piece to the left side of each large side piece. Pin the small divider piece to the center of the large divider piece.

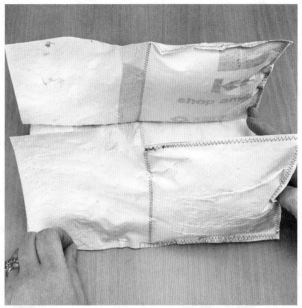

3 For each of the pinned pieces, sew the smaller piece to the larger piece of plastic fabric on three sides, leaving one side open for stuffing. Use unfused plastic scraps to stuff the pieces and then sew the fourth side shut.

4 Pin the large side pieces together so one piece becomes the bottom and the other pieces become the front and back of the bag. The padded sides should all be on the same side. Sew these pieces together where pinned.

5 Pin the padded small bag piece to the padded sides of the front, back and bottom. Pin the unpadded small bag piece to the opposite side. Sew the side pieces to each side of the front, back and bottom piece. It's easier to sew the side bag pieces to the bottom piece first, and then to the front and back pieces. After all the sides have been sewn, trim the edges to create a neater finish.

6 Refer to the striping technique to create a 13" × 12" (33cm × 30cm) striped piece of fused plastic from the colorful plastic packaging.

7 Cut the striped plastic to 11¼" × 11" (29cm × 28cm) to make the bag flap.

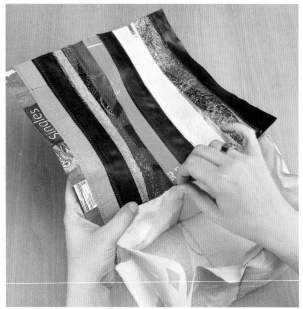

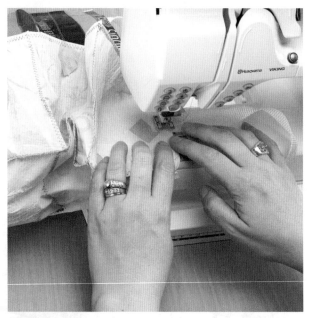

8 Pin one end of the flap to the top of the back piece on the bag and sew together where pinned. Fold the other edge of the flap in ¼" (6mm) and sew down to create a finished edge.

9 Cut 48" (122cm) of white 1" (3cm) nylon webbing. Burn each end of the webbing to prevent raveling. Pin the webbing to the sides of the bag and sew into place. Run across several times for strength.

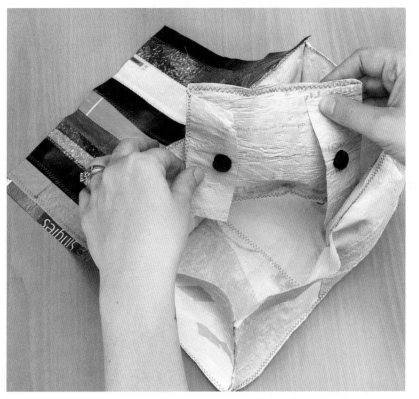

 Adhere Velcro dots to the sides of the padded divider piece. Fasten the divider in the inside of the bag, in the center.

11 Adhere a Velcro dot to each side of the bag flap.

Business Card Holder

Don't keep your business cards in your wallet or back pocket where they might get damaged or wrinkled. Instead, make yourself this handy-dandy business card holder. Not only will everyone be impressed by your business saavy, but they'll think you're the coolest cat on the block with an upcycled card holder!

Techniques used:
Fusing Plastic Bags, page 13
Fabric Appliqué, page 15

Finished measurements:
3¾" × 3½" (10cm × 9cm)

Materials

Plastic
❋ brown shopping bags

Notions
❋ felt scraps
❋ plastic snaps

Tools
❋ iron
❋ ironing board
❋ measuring tape
❋ scissors
❋ sewing machine
❋ snap pliers
❋ straight pins

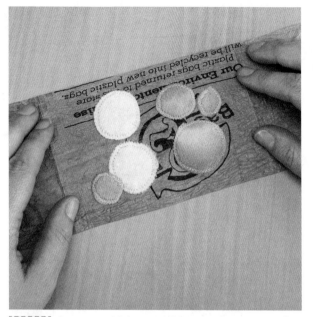

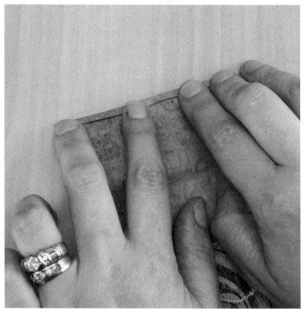

1 Prepare a 10½" × 4" (27cm × 10cm) piece of fused plastic using the brown grocery bags. Refer to the fabric appliqué technique to appliqué felt circles to one side of the plastic.

2 Flip the plastic over. Fold the shorter edges in ¼" (6mm) and sew them down to create finished edges.

3 Fold the shorter sides in 2" (5cm).

4 Sew along the longer sides of the folded plastic to create pockets.

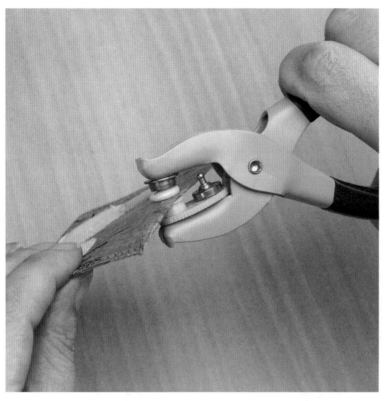

5 Attach plastic snaps to the shorter edges so the holder can snap shut.

tip Snap pliers are a convenient tool for adding snaps to all of your accessories. However, if you don't want to invest in them, you can use a hammer and the setting tool that is usually included with the snaps.

Journal

Everyone needs a journal to write down her random thoughts or jot down important information. This journal is made using scrap paper: junk mail, old bill statements and envelopes. It's practical and easy to make, and can be personalized with plastic appliqué initials for a great last-minute gift.

Techniques used:
Fusing Plastic Bags, page 13
Plastic Appliqué, page 14

Finished measurements:
6" × 4½" (15cm × 11cm)

Materials

Plastic
* ✳ restaurant takeout bag
* ✳ used black garbage bag

Notions
* ✳ corrugated cardboard
* ✳ scrap or recycled paper
* ✳ Velcro dots

Tools
* ✳ iron
* ✳ ironing board
* ✳ measuring tape
* ✳ paper trimmer
* ✳ scissors
* ✳ sewing machine
* ✳ stapler
* ✳ straight pins

1 Prepare a 13½" × 6" (34cm × 15cm) piece of fused plastic from the restaurant takeout bag. Fold the piece in half widthwise. Fold each side in 2¾" (7cm) to create side pockets. Refer to the plastic appliqué instructions to adhere shapes, pictures or letters to the front of the journal using the black garbage bag.

2 Cut a 3" × 1" (8cm × 1cm) piece of fused plastic for the journal closure. Pin the closure to the back cover of the journal, about 2¾" (7cm) from the shorter edge.

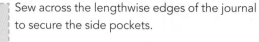

3 Fold each shorter edge in ¼" (6mm) and sew down to create a finished edge. Be careful not to catch the closure when you are sewing across the edge.

4 Sew across the lengthwise edges of the journal to secure the side pockets.

5 Cut an 8" × 5" (20cm × 13cm) piece of corrugated cardboard. Cut pieces of scrap paper to fit against the cardboard backing; pieces should be no longer than 8" (20cm) and no wider than 5" (13cm). With the cardboard at the bottom, fold the pieces in half and trim with a paper cutter on the 5" (13cm) edges so all pages are even lengths. Staple the pages to the cardboard at the center fold.

6 Slide the corrugated cardboard backing into the side pockets of the journal. Adhere a Velcro dot to the closure and front cover.

Envelope

This snazzy little envelope is perfect for keeping important documents like birth certificates or marriage licenses, but it can also be a handy coupon caddy for trips to the supermarket. An eco-minded friend would also appreciate a special letter or invitation in a plastic envelope; she'll be amazed at how colorful and practical it is!

Techniques used:
Fusing Plastic Bags, page 13
Confetti, page 20

Finished measurements:
9" × 4½" (23cm × 11cm)

Materials

Plastic
- ✱ clear plastic bags
- ✱ purple and silver plastic scraps

Notions
- ✱ silver elastic cord

Tools
- ✱ Crop-A-Dile II Big Bite
- ✱ iron
- ✱ ironing board
- ✱ measuring tape
- ✱ scissors
- ✱ sewing machine

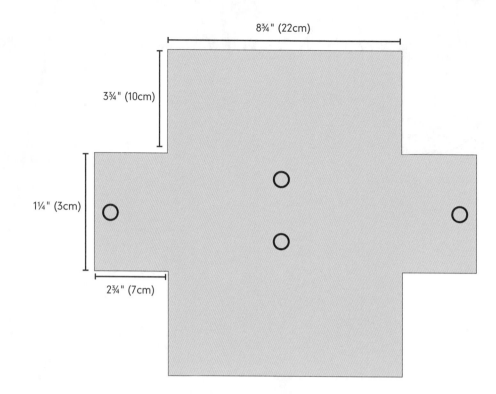

8¾" (22cm)

3¾" (10cm)

1¼" (3cm)

2¾" (7cm)

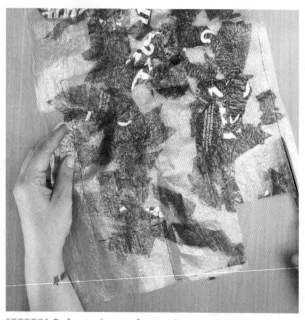

1 Refer to the confetti technique to prepare a piece of fused plastic using the clear plastic bags and the silver and purple scraps. Cut the plastic to the measurements indicated in the diagram above.

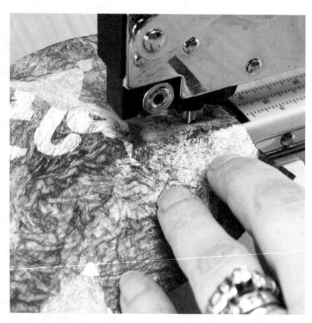

2 Use the Crop-A-Dile tool to punch holes in the fused plastic as shown in the diagram.

3 Sew around the entire envelope to create a neater edge.

4 Thread one 12" (30cm) piece of elastic cord through the center holes in the envelope. Fold the side flaps of the envelope inward.

5 Thread a second 12" (30cm) piece of cord through the holes in the side flaps and tie in the middle. Fold the top and bottom flaps of the envelope inward. Wrap the first piece of elastic cord around the entire folded envelope and tie.

Apron

Be the slickest chick at the summer barbecue with this eco-friendly apron, or whip one up for a friend who's a whiz in the kitchen. The inspiration for this apron came from some friends of mine who eat rabbit, squirrel and deer. I won't eat dinner at their house—they might try to feed me rabbit stew!

Techniques used:
Fusing Plastic Bags, page 13
Stamps, page 24
Stencils, page 23

Finished measurements:
8¼" × 5"
(21cm × 13cm)

Materials

Plastic
* white shopping bags

Notions
* acrylic paint
* ½" (1cm) wide double-fold bias tape
* letter stencils
* rubber stamp
* scrap of ribbon
* StazOn permanent ink

Tools
* iron
* ironing board
* measuring tape
* paintbrush
* scissors
* sewing machine
* straight pins

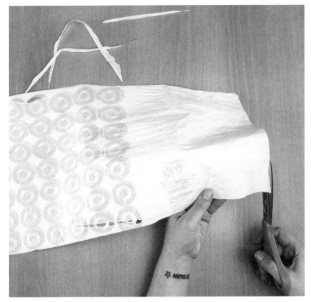

1. Refer to the stamping technique to stamp bunnies or other shapes onto a stack of unfused white shopping bags. Fuse the bags and cut a 24" × 11" (61cm × 28cm) piece of the fused plastic. Cut a heart shape from another piece of fused plastic.

2. Refer to the stencil technique instructions to stencil "What's for Dinner?" or another phrase onto the plastic heart. (If all the words of your phrase don't fit on the heart, you can finish the phrase on the actual apron.)

3. Pin the plastic heart to the front of the apron and sew around the heart to attach. Leave an opening at the top of the heart large enough for a pocket.

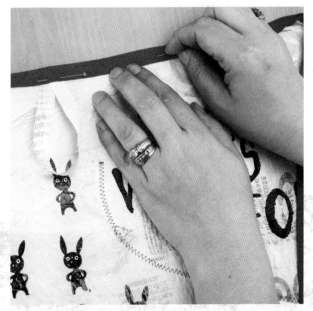

4. Cut 80" (203cm) of ½" (1cm) double-fold bias tape. Pin the tape to the top edge of the apron, leaving excess on each side for the apron strings. Pin a 6" (15cm) piece of ribbon beneath the bias tape in a loop for a towel holder. Sew along the entire strip of bias tape.

Placemats

There are so many options for designing these unique, kid-friendly placemats. Personalize them by collaging a family member's name or favorite foods, or apply a special message. The ideas are endless and will make dinner time fun.

Techniques used:
Fusing Plastic Bags, page 13
Collage, page 19

Finished measurements:
17½" × 14"
(44cm × 36cm)

Materials

Plastic
* colorful plastic packaging
* shopping bags

Notions
* ¼" (6mm) double-fold bias tape

Tools
* iron
* ironing board
* measuring tape
* rotary cutter

* scissors
* sewing machine
* straight edge
* straight pins

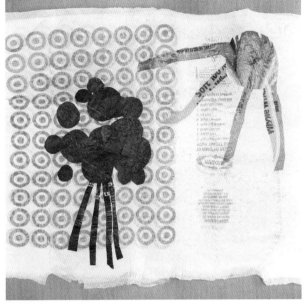

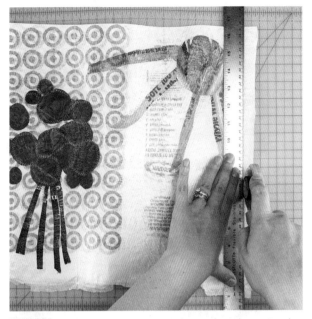

 1 Prepare a 17½" × 14" (44cm × 36cm) piece of fused plastic using the shopping bags. Refer to the collage technique to create a collage on one side of the plastic.

2 Using a rotary cutter and straight edge, trim the edges of the placemat to make them even.

3 Pin the bias tape around the edges of the mat. Sew the tape into place.

Coasters

These coasters will keep those pesky drink rings from forming on your coffee table. Don't limit your design to the pattern shown here; use your imagination to create custom coaster sets to match the decor in your home!

Techniques used:
Fusing Plastic Bags, page 13
Collage, page 19

Finished measurements:
4½" × 4½"
(11cm × 11cm)

Materials

Plastic
* colorful plastic packaging
* shopping bags

Notions
* ¼" (6mm) double-fold bias tape
* felt

Tools
* iron
* ironing board
* measuring tape
* rotary cutter

* scissors
* sewing machine
* straight edge
* straight pins

1 Prepare a piece of fused plastic from the shopping bags. Refer to the collage technique to create a collage on one side of the plastic.

2 Place the plastic on top of a piece of felt. Using a rotary cutter and straight edge, cut the plastic and felt to 4¼" × 4¼" (11cm × 11cm).

3 Pin the piece of felt to the wrong side of the coaster. Pin the bias tape around the edges of the coaster and felt. Sew the tape into place.
Repeat Steps 1–3 as many times as you like to make a set of coasters.

Makeup Pouch

These pouches are perfect for makeup or toiletries. I want to make a bunch to organize my hall closet so I can actually find what I'm looking for when I'm getting ready in the morning. Best of all, if something spills inside the bag, you can simply wipe it clean. Don't you just love plastic?

Technique used:
Tulle, page 18

Finished measurements:
7" × 6½" (18cm × 17cm)

Materials

Plastic
* ❋ clear plastic bags
* ❋ pink tulle

Notions
* ❋ 7" (18cm) zipper

Tools
* ❋ ink pen
* ❋ iron
* ❋ ironing board
* ❋ measuring tape
* ❋ scissors
* ❋ sewing machine
* ❋ straight edge
* ❋ straight pins
* ❋ zipper foot attachment

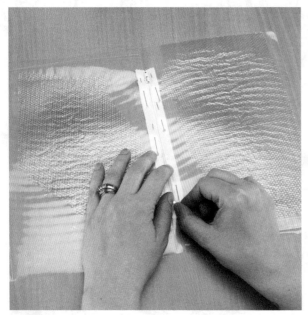

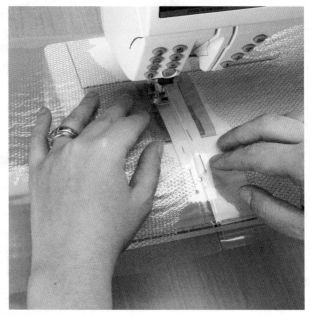

1 Refer to the tulle technique to prepare two 9" × 9" (23cm × 23cm) pieces of fused plastic from the clear bags and tulle. Pin the zipper to the plastic, centering the zipper on the edge of each piece.

2 Using the zipper foot attachment, sew the zipper onto both pieces of fused plastic.

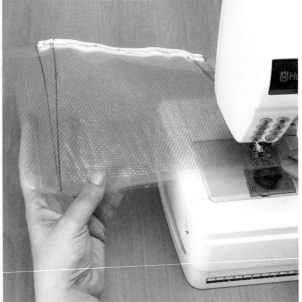

3 Fold the entire piece in half along the zipper, right sides together. The outer part of the zipper will be facing down. Draw a straight line (Line A) with the pen from the end of the zipper fabric to the bottom edge of the fused plastic. Repeat for the other side.

4 Draw an angled line (Line B) from the end of the zipper teeth to where Line A ends. Repeat for the other side. Unzip the zipper almost completely before sewing. Sew along Line B on both sides. Sew along the bottom edge.

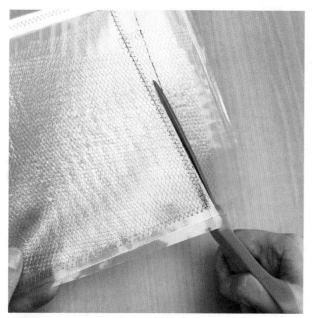

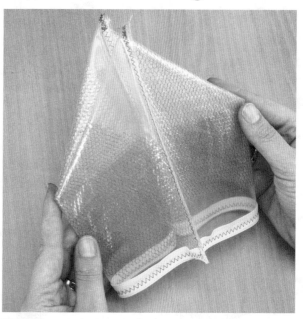

5 Trim the edges of the fused plastic to within ¼" (6mm) of the seams.

6 Turn the bag upside down. Fold the bag so the corners form two points on the bottom.

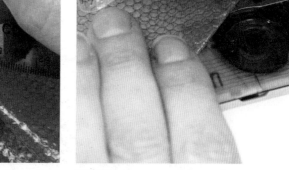

7 Measure 1" (3cm) down from each point and mark with a pen.

8 Sew across the mark to create a small triangle at each point. Cut off the points to within ¼" (6mm) of the seam. Turn the bag right side out.

Shower Essentials Caddy

I designed this waterproof shower caddy so I always know where my special hair products are when they're not in use. This caddy is also great for camping; my daughter takes one with her to Girl Scout camp every year.

Techniques used:
Fusing Plastic Bags, page 13
Confetti, page 20

Finished measurements:
8½" × 6½" × 5½" (22cm × 17cm × 14cm)

Materials

Plastic
※ clear plastic bags
※ flagging tape

Notions
※ plastic snap fasteners

Tools
※ iron
※ ironing board
※ measuring tape
※ pencil
※ scissors
※ sewing machine
※ snap pliers
※ straight pins

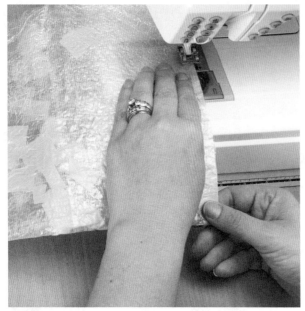

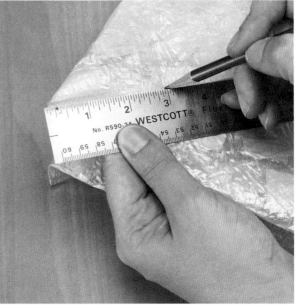

 Refer to the confetti technique to prepare pieces of fused plastic in the following sizes: 19" × 13" (48cm × 33cm) for the main bag and two 16½" × 1" (42cm × 3cm) for the handles. Fold the main bag in half widthwise, right sides facing. Sew along both edges.

 Fold the bag so the corners form two points on the bottom. Measure 3" (8cm) down from each point and mark with a pencil.

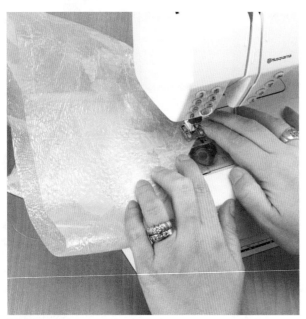

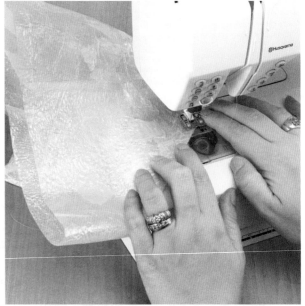

 Sew across each mark to create a triangle at each point. Cut off each triangle within ¼" (6mm) of the seam. Turn the bag right side out.

 Fold the top edges of the bag in ¼" (6mm) and pin. As you pin, attach a 6" (15cm) thin strip of fused plastic in a loop for a razor holder Sew down the folds and the loop to create a finished edge.

5 Pin a handle to each side of the bag and sew into place, running over it several times for added strength.

Mini Project: Soap Bag

1. Cut a 10½" x 5" (27cm × 13cm) piece of fused plastic. Fold the shorter edges in ¼" (6mm) and sew down to create a finished edge.

2. Fold the bag in half widthwise, right sides together. Sew the sides together (see Figure 1).

3. Fold the bag so the corners form two points on the bottom. Measure 1" (3cm) down from each point and mark. Sew across each mark to create a triangle at each point. Cut off each triangle within ¼" (6mm) of the seam. Turn the bag right side out.

4. Attach a snap closure to one side of the soap caddy (see Figure 2). Attach the other snap to the inside of the shower essentials bag.

Figure 1

Figure 2

Shower Cap

Did you know it's actually healthier for your hair to skip the shampoo from time to time? On days when you'd rather keep your locks dry, why not use this fabulous shower cap? I wear mine around the house just because I can—you should try it!

Techniques used:
Fusing Plastic Bags, page 13; Confetti, page 20

Finished Measurement:
16" (41cm) base circumference, unstretched

Materials

Plastic
* clear plastic bags
* flagging tape

Notions
* elastic tape

Tools
* iron
* ironing board
* sewing machine
* scissors
* measuring tape

1 Refer to the confetti technique to prepare a 19" × 19" (48cm) square of fused plastic. Cut an 18" (46cm) diameter circle from the plastic. Measure and cut a piece of elastic that fits snugly around your forehead.

2 Position the elastic 1" (3cm) from the edge of the circle but do not pin it on. As you sew the elastic on, stretch the elastic taut and scrunch up the plastic underneath, creating a bunched-up effect. Keep the elastic consistently 1" (3cm) from the edge of the circle. Trim any excess elastic and turn the cap so the elastic is on the inside.

Shower Slippers

These stylish handmade shower shoes have several different uses. Wear them while you mop the floors, slide them on before taking out the trash or use them to keep your feet clean and germ-free in the communal shower at camp.

Technique used:
Fusing Plastic Bags, page 13
Confetti, page 20

Finished measurements:
11" × 4½"
(28cm × 11cm)

Materials

Plastic
* clear plastic bags
* flagging tape
* white shopping bags

Notions
* grommets

* nonslip rubber strips with adhesive backing

Tools
* Crop-A-Dile II Big Bite or grommet tool
* iron
* ironing board

* measuring tape
* scissors
* straight pins
* thin cardboard

Template
* shower slipper top, page 123

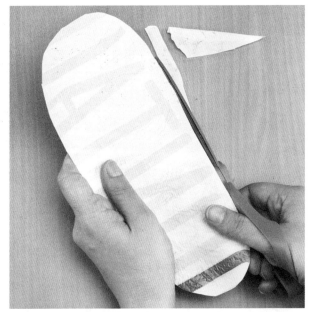

1 Trace your foot shape onto a piece of thin cardboard, making the shape ¼" (6mm) larger all around. Cut out the shape. Prepare a piece of fused plastic from the white shopping bags. Cut two foot shapes from the plastic.

2 Refer to the confetti technique to prepare a piece of fused plastic from the clear bags and flagging tape. Use the template to cut two slipper tops from the plastic. Pin them to the top piece of the foot shape. At the notches in the slipper top edges, overlap the plastic as you pin to create a domelike shape.

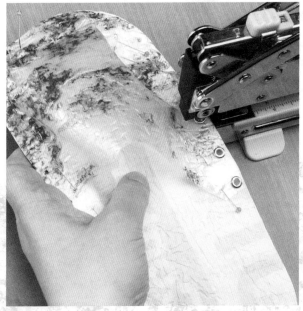

3 Starting where the top piece overlaps the foot piece, punch ³/₁₆" (2mm) grommet holes with the Crop-A-Dile II tool, positioning the holes about 1" (3cm) apart and ¼" (6mm) from the edge.

4 Using the setter on the Crop-A-Dile II or a grommet tool, insert ³/₁₆" (2mm) grommets into the holes. Adhere a nonslip rubber strip to the bottom of the slipper. Repeat Steps 2–4 for the other slipper.

Clothing Caddy

Use this clothing caddy to keep your clothes dry while you shower. When you're ready to get dressed, flip the top and hang up the bag for easier access to your undies. This bag is great for camp or the college dorm—anywhere you don't have a place to keep your clean clothes dry while you get clean.

Techniques used:
Fusing Plastic Bags, page 13
Striping, page 25

Finished measurements:
8¼" × 5"
(21cm × 13cm)

Materials

Plastic
* colorful plastic packaging
* white shopping bags

Notions
* grommets
* 1" (3cm) nylon webbing
* Velcro dots

Tools
* Crop-A-Dile II Big Bite
* hammer
* iron
* ironing board
* measuring tape
* pencil
* scissors
* sewing machine
* straight pins

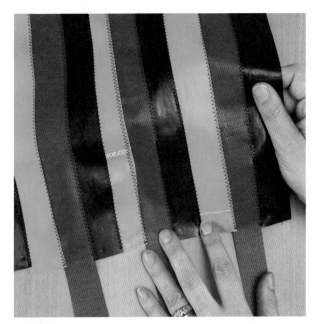

1 Prepare two 19" × 14½" (48cm × 37cm) bag pieces of fused plastic using the white shopping bags.

2 Refer to the striping technique instructions to create a 13" × 11" (33cm × 28cm) bag flap.

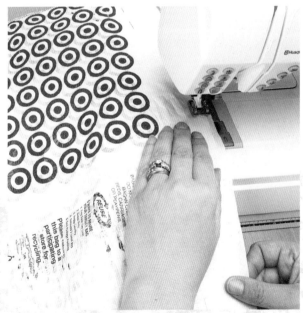

3 Center and pin the striped plastic piece to one bag piece on the long side. Sew the bag flap to the wrong side of the bag piece.

4 Pin the two bag pieces with the right sides together. Sew the edges together, using a ¼" (6mm) seam allowance. Leave the top unsewn.

5 Fold the bag so the corners form two points at the bottom. Measure 3" (8cm) from each point and mark with a pencil.

6 Sew across the mark to create a triangle at each point. Cut off the triangles within ¼" (6mm) of the seam. Turn the bag right side out.

7 Sew across the edge of the striped piece to create a neater finish.

8 Using the Crop-A-Dile II tool, punch grommet holes into the top corners of the back bag piece. Add grommets to the corners using a hammer or grommet tool.

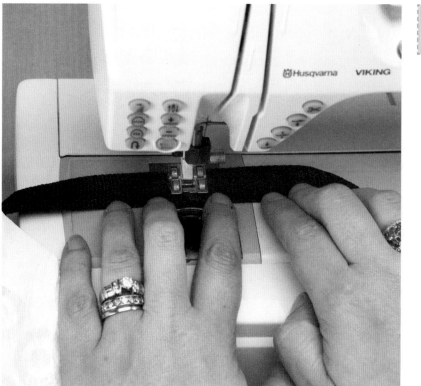

 9 Thread a 40" (102cm) piece of 1" (3cm) nylon webbing through one of the grommets and then through the other grommet. Sew the two ends of the webbing together to connect them in a loop.

 tip The striping is a great way to use up your scraps. Experiment with different plastic packaging to achieve a rainbow effect!

Travel Pouch

When my family is planning a trip, it seems like we have an endless mountain of papers; plane tickets, passports, and hotel confirmations are just the start of it. I came up with this travel pouch so we could stay organized and focus on having fun.

Techniques used:
Fusing Plastic Bags, page 13
Fabric Appliqué, page 15

Finished measurements:
17½" × 14" (44cm × 36cm)

Materials

Plastic
* plastic tablecloth without felt backing

Notions
* felt scraps
* 14" (36cm) zipper

Tools
* iron
* ironing board

* measuring tape
* scissors
* sewing machine
* straight pins
* zipper foot attachment

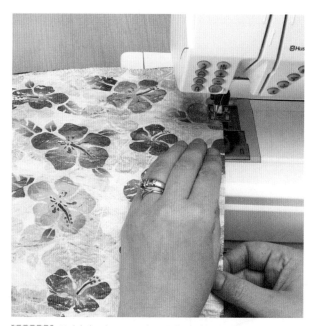

1 Prepare two 12½" × 12" (32cm × 32cm) pieces of fused plastic using the tablecloth. (Fuse together two layers of tablecloth for each piece.) Refer to the fabric appliqué technique instructions to sew felt letters to the front of one of the pieces.

Pin the wrong sides of the front and back of the travel pouch to the right side of the zipper. Trim the zipper to fit the plastic pieces. Using the zipper foot attachment, sew the zipper into place.

2 Fold the bag so the right sides are facing. Unzip the zipper almost all the way before sewing. Sew around the edges of the bag. Turn the bag right side out.

tip When scrounging up materials for this project, make sure your recycled tablecloth doesn't have a felt backing. This would keep the plastic from fusing properly and would probably result in a burned and melted mess!

Bucket Hat

Stay on the cutting edge of fashion with this super-cute bucket hat. If you're always getting caught in the rain without an umbrella, this hat will keep your hair dry and prevent the evils of frizz!

Technique used:
Fusing Plastic Bags, page 13

Finished measurement:
27½" (70cm) base circumference

Materials

Plastic
* floral: plastic tablecloth
* green: thick plastic shopping bag

Notions
* ¼" (6mm) double-fold bias tape

Tools
* iron
* ironing board
* scissors
* sewing machine
* straight pins

Templates
* bucket hat side, page 122
* bucket hat top, page 122

1 Prepare a piece of green fused plastic and a piece of floral fused plastic. Use the templates to cut two side pieces from the green plastic and one top piece from the floral plastic. When cutting from the template shapes, the plastic should be doubled, with a fold on one side. (This is indicated on the template.)

2 Pin the curved edges of the side pieces to the longer sides of the top piece. Sew the pieces together where pinned. Turn the top of the hat so the seams are on the inside.

3 Pin ¼" (6mm) double-fold bias tape around the edges of the hat. Sew the tape into place.

Mini Project: Plastic Flower

Materials: unfused plastic bags
Tools: circular mini-loom; yarn needle; Quick Grip adhesive or pin backing

1. Cut a 6' (2m) long, ½" (1cm) wide strip of plastic from an unfused plastic bag. (For an unbroken strip, start at the top of the bag and cut around the edge continuously until you reach the bottom.) Cut a second strip of unfused plastic about 12" (30cm) for sewing (see Figure 1).

2. Using a circular mini loom, weave figure-eights around adjacent pegs to create a flower shape. Repeat this weaving to make a second layer of plastic in the same pattern (see Figure 2).

3. Thread 12" (30cm) of the plastic yarn through a large plastic needle and sew through the center of the flower several times to secure it, pulling the needle through different places in the center each time (see Figure 3). Remove the flower from the loom. Tie off and trim the strip of plastic used to sew the flower.

4. Attach the flower to a bag or a hat with a dot of Quick Grip, or attach a pin backing to the flower to wear it as a pin (see Figure 4).

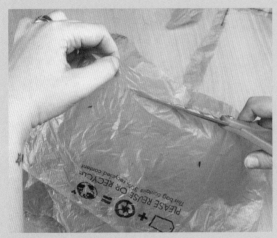

Figure 1

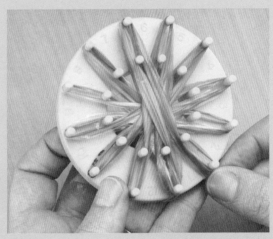

Figure 2

Figure 3

Figure 4

Party Hat

Party time! Throw a recycling-themed party and make these party hats for the guests. No one will suspect they're made from trash, but everyone will certainly look fabulous!

Techniques used:
Fusing Plastic Bags, page 13; Paints, page 21

Finished measurements:
20"(51cm) base circumference

Materials

Plastic
* brown shopping bags
* white shopping bags

Notions
* acrylic paint
* clear sealer

* double-sided tape
* glass glitter
* Quick Grip adhesive

Tools
* iron
* ironing board

* measuring tape
* paintbrush
* pen
* scissors
* straight edge

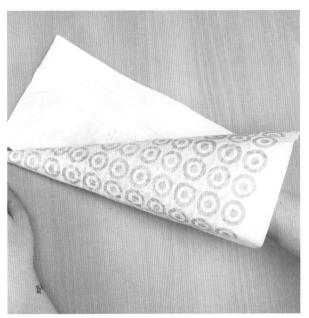

 Prepare a 19" × 16" (48cm × 41cm) piece of fused plastic using the white shopping bags.

2 Starting from one corner, roll the plastic fabric so it forms a cone shape. One end will be pointed and tight, while the other will be open.

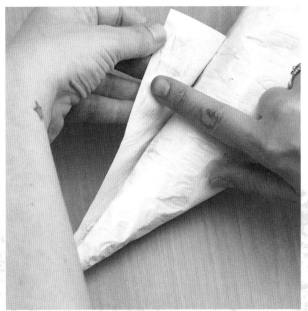

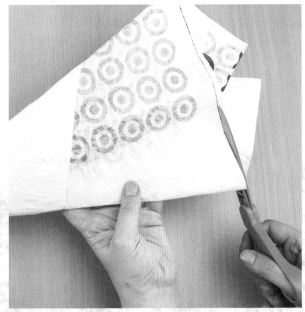

3 After the end of the plastic is rolled, secure it with a piece of double-sided tape.

4 Use a straight edge to draw a straight line at the bottom of the hat. Cut along this line.

5 Refer to the paints technique to paint the outside of the hat with acrylic paint.

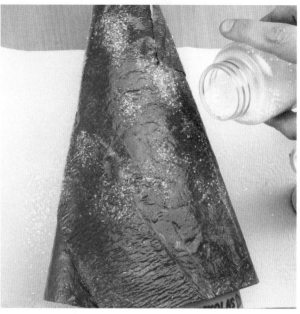

6 Sprinkle glass glitter onto the wet paint. Let it dry.

7 While the paint is drying, make seven to eight small pom-poms and one large pom-pom using the brown grocery bags (see *Mini Project: Pom-poms* on the next page). After the paint is dry, adhere the small pom-poms around the base of the hat and the large pom-pom to the tip with Quick Grip. Coat the hat and the pom-poms in clear sealer. Sprinkle glass glitter over the pom-poms while the sealer is still wet.

Mini Project: Pom-poms

1. Cut ¼" (6mm) strips from a stack of unfused plastic bags (see Figure 1). Each strip will be a loop.

2. Gather six loops. Fold the loops in half and then fold again (see Figure 2).

3. Tie a separate strip around the folded loops (see Figure 3).

4. Cut through the loops to create the fringe (see Figure 4). Trim the fringe on the pom-pom as desired to make larger or smaller pom-poms.

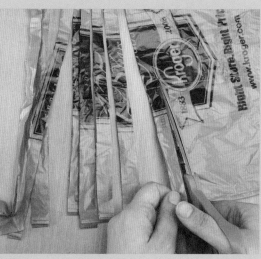

Figure 1

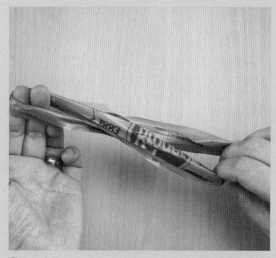

Figure 2

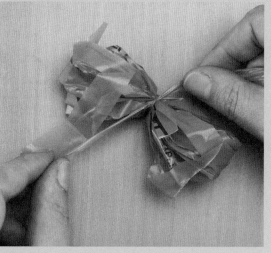

Figure 3

Figure 4

Cowboy Hat

This Western-style hat is great for theme parties, costumes or even Hat Day at the office. If you're feeling super-creative, you could make an entire outfit from plastic and go as the "Plastic Cowboy" for Halloween next year! Ride 'em, cowboy!

Techniques used:
Fusing Plastic Bags, page 13
Crayon Shavings, page 16

Finished measurement:
22" (56cm) base circumference

Materials

Plastic
※ blue snack packaging
※ clear plastic bags

Notions
※ crayon shavings

Tools
※ iron
※ ironing board
※ measuring tape
※ scissors
※ sewing machine
※ straight pins

Templates
※ cowboy hat brim, page 121
※ cowboy hat side, page 120

1 Refer to the crayon shavings technique instructions to prepare a piece of fused plastic using the clear bags. Prepare a piece of fused plastic using the snack packaging. Cut two side pieces and one brim piece from the clear plastic using the templates. Cut one 25½" × 2" (65cm × 5cm) piece for the hat band and one 15" × 4¼" (38cm × 11cm) piece for the hat top from the blue plastic. When cutting the template shapes, the plastic should be doubled, with a fold on one side. (This is indicated on the template.)

2 Pin the curved edges of the side pieces to the longer sides of the top piece, right sides together. Sew the pieces together where pinned. Turn the top of the hat so the seams are on the inside.

3 Pin the hat band around the top of the hat and sew into place. Sew the hat band ends together after it is connected to the top of the hat.

4 Sew the ends of the brim together.

tip

Don't let your brim pucker! It's sometimes difficult to get the brim to lay correctly the first time; sometimes the brim is a little too big or too small for the hat. Don't be afraid to readjust the placement of the brim or trim the brim as needed.

5 Fit the brim over the hat, sliding it down to the edge of the hat band. Pin the brim into place. Sew the brim onto the hat and flip the brim edges upward.

Queenie Crown

Be a queen for a day—or a lifetime! My nickname is "Queenie," but while I'm at work, I have to wear an invisible crown. Once I'm at home, though, I can put on my recycled crown for all to see and admire!

Technique used:
Fusing Plastic Bags, page 13
Fabric Appliqué, page 15
Paint, page 21

Finished measurements:
15½" × 5½" (39cm × 14cm)

Materials

Plastic
※ white shopping bags

Notions
※ acrylic paint
※ felt scraps
※ metal bottle cap
※ needle and thread

※ pom-pom trim
※ various recycled embellishments

Tools
※ awl
※ hammer
※ iron

※ ironing board
※ measuring tape
※ paintbrush
※ scissors
※ sewing machine
※ straight pins

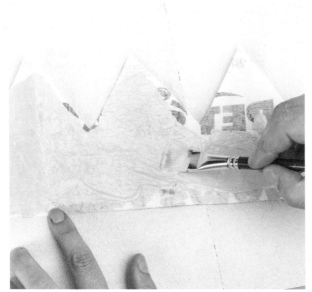

 1 Prepare a 15" × 7" (38cm × 18cm) piece of fused plastic using the white shopping bags. Draw a crown shape across the plastic and cut it out. Refer to the paints technique to paint the crown shape on one side with acrylic paint. Let the paint dry.

2 Refer to the fabric appliqué technique to sew numbers, words or a name onto the painted side of the crown shape.

3 Sew embellishments such as plastic pom-poms (see page 105), pom-pom trim, buttons or rickrack onto the crown. Sew several strands of ribbon at least 12" (30cm) long onto the bottom corner of the crown.

 4 Use a hammer and awl to punch a hole into the center of a metal bottle cap. Using needle and thread, sew the bottle cap to the side opposite the hanging ribbons. To wear, wrap one of the ribbons around the back part of your head. Wrap the ribbon around the bottle cap a few times to secure.

Robot Plushie

This lovable little robot will steal your heart. He's great for introducing little ones to the advantages of recycling and will provide hours of eco-minded fun. Making a plushie is also a great way to use up unfused plastic scraps.

Techniques used:
Fusing Plastic Bags, page 13
Paints, page 21

Finished measurements:
11" × 11"
(28cm × 28cm)

Materials

Plastic
* ✳ unfused plastic scraps
* ✳ white shopping bags

Notions
* ✳ Quick Grip adhesive
* ✳ red felt scrap
* ✳ silver acrylic paint

Tools
* ✳ iron
* ✳ ironing board
* ✳ measuring tape
* ✳ paintbrush
* ✳ permanent marker
* ✳ scissors
* ✳ sewing maching
* ✳ straight pins

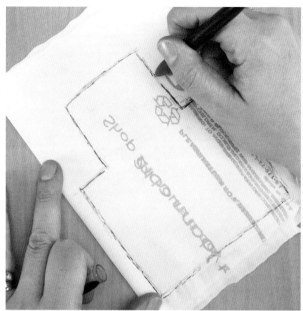

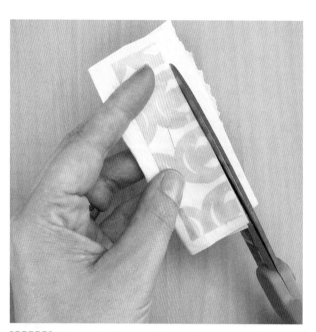

1. Prepare a piece of fused plastic using the shopping bags. Sketch a robot body onto the piece of fused plastic. Cut out two identical body shapes: a front and a back.

2. Cut eight 4" × 1" (10cm × 3cm) pieces from a piece of fused plastic for the the arms and legs.

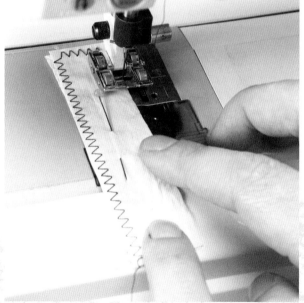

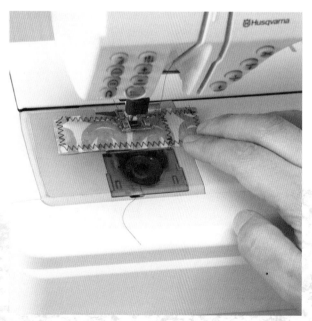

3. Sew two arm pieces together on three sides, leaving one side open for stuffing. Stuff the arm with unfused plastic scraps, and then sew it shut on the fourth side.

4. Sew across the arm and through the stuffing in two places on the arm to create "joints." Repeat Steps 3 and 4 for the other arm and both legs.

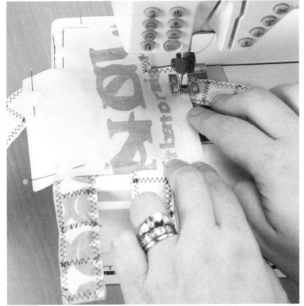

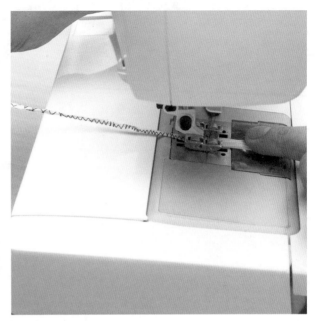

 5 Slip the robot's arms and legs between the front and back pieces and pin them into place. Sew around the entire robot body to attach them and join the front and back of the robot's body. Do not sew the top of the head; leave it open for stuffing. Stuff the robot with unfused plastic scraps.

6 Twist a 5½" (14cm) scrap piece of unfused plastic and zigzag stitch through it. Fold the piece in half. This is the robot's antenna.

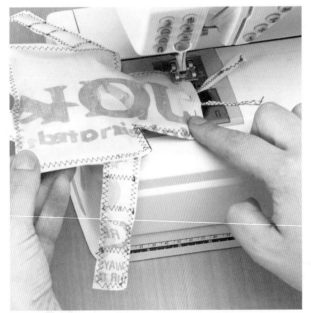

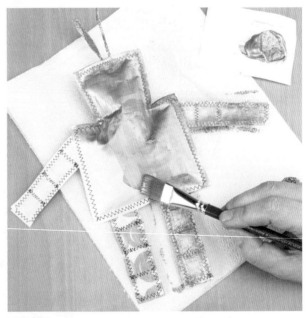

7 Fold the antenna in half and place it just inside the head. Sew the head shut.

 8 Refer to the paints technique to paint the robot with metallic silver acrylic paint. Let the paint dry.

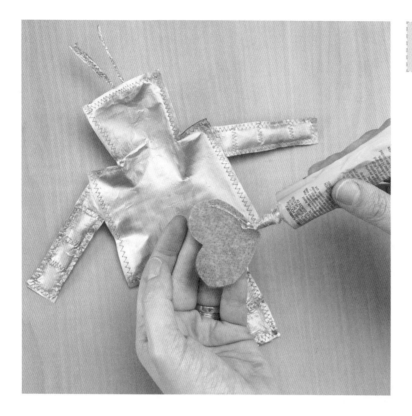

9 Cut a heart from red felt and adhere it to the front of the robot with Quick Grip.

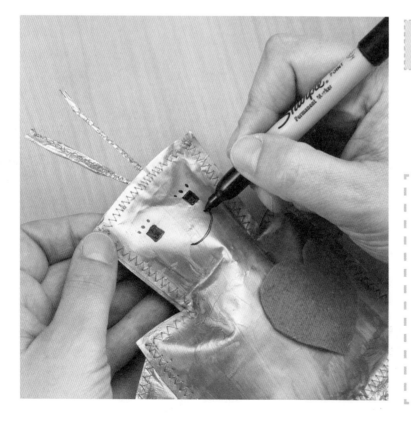

10 Draw a face onto the robot with a permanent marker.

♻ tip

For a "wish plushie," don't glue down the top of the heart. This will make it a pocket to tuck a written wish inside.

Gallery

Owl and Bunny Plushies

Pringles and Bullseye Wallets

Flower Petal Business Card Holder

hawkins@one.net
hawkinsandhawkins.biz

Folio Folder

Bird Coasters

Tote Bags

Heart Apron

Hot Dog Buns Apron

Templates

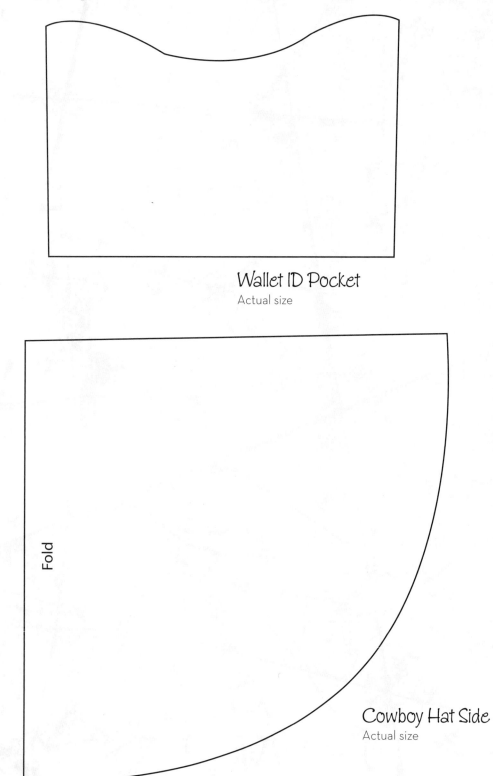

Wallet ID Pocket
Actual size

Fold

Cowboy Hat Side
Actual size

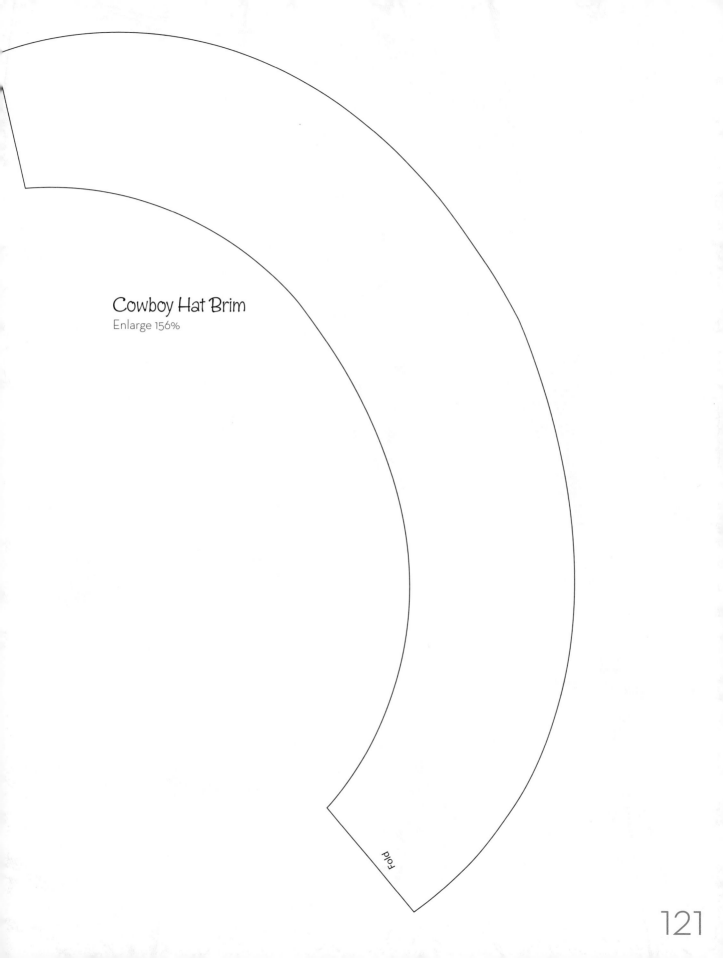

Cowboy Hat Brim

Enlarge 156%

Fold

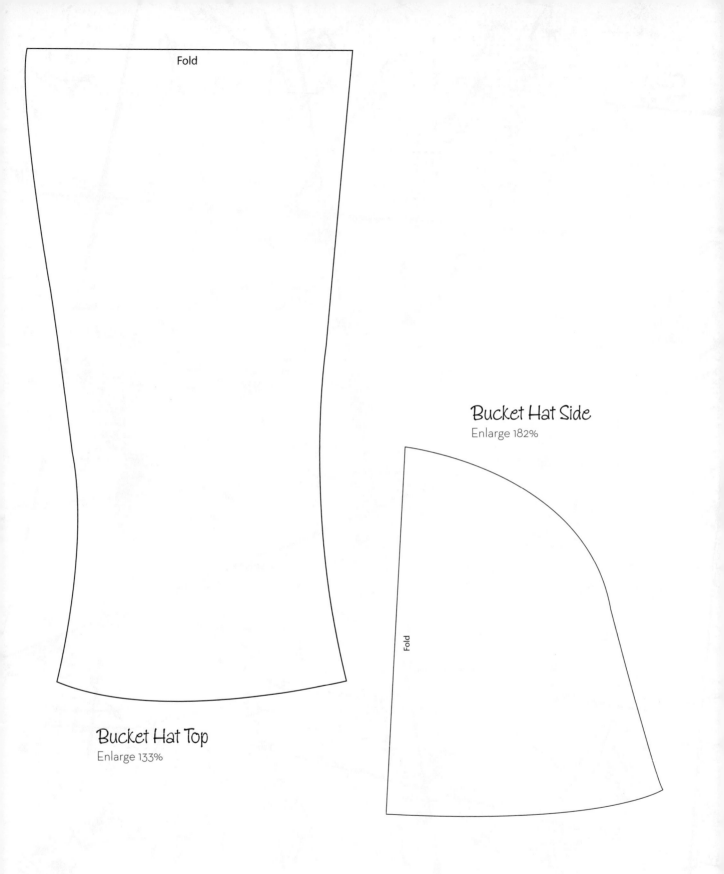

Fold

Bucket Hat Side
Enlarge 182%

Fold

Bucket Hat Top
Enlarge 133%

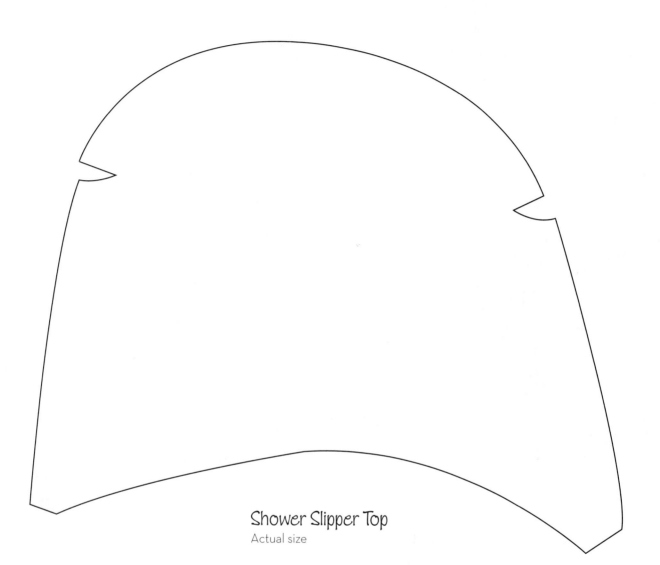

Shower Slipper Top
Actual size

Clutch Form

Enlarge 125%

Clutch Pocket
Actual size

Index

You don't have to stop here—keep crafting with these other titles from North Light Books

Heidi Boyd
Recycle, Reuse, Recraft! *Craftcycle* is the creative crafter's way to recycle and reuse everyday items destined for the trash bin. Recycle magazine pages into a decorative bowl or trash basket, reuse scrap wood in a beautiful birdhouse, or recraft broken china into a mosaic flower pot! Tips, techniques and more than forty projects help you get the most out of every season while impacting the environment the least. Craft your way into a greener life!

paperback, 144 pages
ISBN-10: 1-60061-304-7
ISBN-13: 978-1-60061-304-3
Z2888

Micaela Preston
Practically Green will show you how to make smart, healthy purchases for your family without spending tedious hours researching the pros and cons of all the products available on the market today. Features include clip-out checklists for you to reference while shopping and recipes for non-toxic cleaning products and luxurious, homemade beauty products.

paperback, 224 pages
ISBN-10: 1-60061-329-2
ISBN-13: 978-1-60061-329-6
Z2972

Alisa Burke
Learn how to bring graffiti art off the street and onto canvas to make everything from wall hangings to bracelets and bags. Inside *Canvas Remix*, you'll find more than 40 techniques for combining paint, collage and canvas in totally unexpected ways. Creating graffiti-inspired art may not give you instant street cred, but once you've mastered these techniques, your finished pieces are sure to turn heads.

paperback, 128 pages
ISBN-10: 1-60061-075-7
ISBN-13: 978-1-60061-075-2
Z1844

These and other fine North Light titles are available at your local craft retailer, bookstore or online supplier, or visit our Web site at www.mycraftivitystore.com.